Shaping Future Defense Budgets

Richard L. Kugler and Hans Binnendijk

Center for Technology and National Security Policy

National Defense University

November 2004

Hans Binnendijk holds the Roosevelt Chair of National Security Policy at the National Defense University and is Director of the Center for Technology and National Security Policy. He previously served on the National Security Council as Special Assistant to the President and Senior Director for Defense Policy and Arms Control (1999-2001). From 1994 to 1999, Dr. Binnendijk was Director of the Institute for National Strategic Studies at the National Defense University. Prior to that he was Principal Deputy Director of the State Department Policy Planning Staff (1993-1994).

Richard L. Kugler is a Distinguished Research Professor at the Center for Technology and National Security Policy, where he performs analyses. His specialty is U.S. defense strategy, global security affairs, and NATO. He advises senior echelons of the Office of Secretary of Defense, the Joint Staff, and the interagency community. He has been an analyst and senior executive in the Office of Secretary of Defense for Program Analysis and Evaluation (1975-1984), Director of DOD Strategic Concepts and Development Center (1984-1988), and Research Leader at RAND (1988-1997). He is author of multiple books, journal articles, and official studies on U.S. defense strategy and programs as well as NATO and global security affairs.

Defense & Technology Papers *are published by the National Defense University Center for Technology and National Security Policy, Fort Lesley J. McNair, Washington, DC. CTNSP publications are available online at* http://www.ndu.edu/ctnsp/publications.html.

Contents

Executive Summary

This paper assesses key issues in U.S. defense spending in the next decade and is intended to serve as a guide to analyzing the fiscal year 2006 budget submission. Wartime expenses aside, the big spending increases of recent years seem unlikely to be repeated far into the future. Persistent federal deficits and growing domestic entitlement programs will constrain the amount of money that can be spent on military preparedness. The defense budget may level off just as it should rise to accommodate high operating costs and mounting requirements for military transformation. If so, budget constraints will compel a concerted effort to spend available defense funds as wisely as possible. Spending patterns and priorities will change, and tradeoffs will be necessary.

If pressures on the defense budget increase, the biggest challenge facing the Department of Defense (DOD) will be determining how best to pursue two key transformation goals. The first goal is strengthening ground forces and related joint capabilities for expeditionary operations along the "southern arc of instability" in the near to mid term. The second goal is enhancing strategic dominance over future peer adversaries over the long term through acquisition of new platforms, space systems, and similar high-tech assets. Within this framework, DOD will need to address other weighty issues. Should investments in ground forces increase? If so, what priorities should be pursued? Can savings be extracted from support programs and from the operations and maintenance (O&M) budget to help fund investments? If so, how? Should spending on basic research increase? If so, can development of new technologies be accelerated while controlling costs? How should scarce procurement funds be allocated among new weapons emerging from research, development, testing, and evaluation? What is the best budget strategy for the long haul? Should the U.S. government create an overall national security budget for the interagency community?

Careful analysis of each of these issues is necessary, individually and collectively. The budget and program decisions flowing from the analysis will have major implications for future U.S. forces. This study recommends focusing on enhancing expeditionary warfare capabilities, while not denuding long-term transformation. In particular, it argues that, if DOD is to pursue ambitious transformation plans for both goals, it will need to find savings elsewhere.

Introduction

This analysis focuses on the basic U.S. defense budget—subfunction 051 of the President's budget—which provides for normal peacetime military preparedness but not for extra wartime costs in Iraq and Afghanistan. A sense of strategic perspective is needed on where the U.S. defense budget and program are headed because decisions with enduring consequences lie just ahead. A political consensus has been reached in recent years on the need to increase defense spending to strengthen U.S. security, to transform the U.S. military for the Information Age, and, since September 11, 2001, to wage a Global War on Terrorism (GWOT). As a result, the defense budget rose from $290 billion in 2000 to $402.6 billion for 2005, even before the supplemental requests for Afghanistan and Iraq. By 2009, the defense budget is projected to rise to nearly $500 billion. But pressures are growing to curtail defense spending.

The Department of Defense (DOD) budget began growing in the late 1990s, rising (in current dollars) from $258 billion in 1998 to $290 billion in 2000 to $346 billion in 2002. The increases bolstered defense preparedness and promoted force transformation. Unfortunately, the defense budget is unlikely to continue growing at the rate of 3-5 percent annual real increases of the recent past. This especially could be true after 2010. A recent study by the Congressional Budget Office (CBO) forecasts only a total 3-4 percent increase in real defense spending *over the entire period 2010-2022.* [1] That amounts to about one-third of 1 percent per year.

A stagnant defense budget coupled with rising costs could create annual shortfalls of $15-80 billion. Obviously, DOD will not be able to fund all plausible requirements, and tough choices about defense strategy, force structure, priorities, and risks will be necessary.

Uncertain Top Lines

A sense of drama is beginning to surround the topic of future defense budgets. The defense budget "train wreck," predicted in the 1990s, was only postponed, not avoided. There are several interacting trends that point toward imminent problems.

First, wartime costs for Iraq and Afghanistan have been funded by special supplemental appropriations that enable DOD to continue focusing the basic defense budget on the standard tasks of peacetime military preparedness. Whether supplemental appropriations will continue to be funded is unclear. If they fail to cover all wartime costs, DOD will have to dip into its basic budget.

Second, even if future supplemental appropriations are adequate, prospects for sustained real increases in defense spending are clouded by larger trends facing the federal budget. Persistent federal deficits coupled with big increases in entitlement programs—e.g., costs for social security and health care could double in the next 10-15 years—are likely to constrain the amount of money available for national defense.

---

[1] Congressional Budget Office, *The Long Term Implications of Current Defense Plans: Summary Update for Fiscal Year 2005* (Washington, DC: Government Printing Office, 2004).

Third, these constraints will take effect at a time when requirements for defense budgets are rising to fund not only growing daily expenses for personnel and operations, but also big increases in procurement budgets for both long-delayed modernization and transformation of all services. These trends, which are dramatically different from those of recent years, promise to complicate the task of forging defense budgets.

The prospect of mounting budgetary pressures on defense planning over the long term provides a frame of reference for judging the significance of where the defense "top line"—total funding for each budget—seems headed in the near term. In February 2004, the Bush Administration sent a request to Congress for a FY 2005 defense budget of $402.6 billion in budget authority (BA) and $429.6 billion in outlays. The BA request was $23 billion higher than the request for FY 2004. Such increases are unlikely to continue for long.

Since 2000, one-third of the increase from $290.5 billion to $402.6 billion was needed to offset inflation; the remaining two-thirds ($73.8 billion) provided real growth. Through 2009, about one-half of the projected growth to $488.9 billion will be needed for inflation; the remainder will provide additional real growth of about $40.4 billion. After 2009, further increases will depend on decisions regarding inflation and real growth. By 2015, the budget could rise to $550-600 billion or more, but future top lines are uncertain. As history shows, big defense spending increases typically last only a few years, then are replaced by periods of leveling off.

Budgetary data for this study are taken mainly from DOD's "Green Book" (*National Defense Budget Estimates for FY2005*) and related documents published by the Pentagon Comptroller. Table 1 shows how defense budget requests and forecasts have evolved since the 2002 budget of $345.6 billion. The "budget request and forecast" shows the figures submitted by the Bush Administration for the basic defense budget (051). The chart also shows actual defense spending for 2003 and 2004, which was higher than original requests because of the interaction of Congressional alterations and wartime supplemental appropriations. In fiscal year 2003, Congress approved $62.4 billion for wartime spending. In 2004, supplemental appropriations totaled $68 billion. Congress also passed a bridging allocation for combat operations of $25 billion in August of 2004. Press reports indicate that a fiscal year 2005 supplemental request of up to $70 billion is being prepared. For this analysis, the key is the original budget request and projection for 2005, which shows the forecasted rise from $402.6 billion in 2005 to $488.9 billion in 2009. The DOD budget request for 2005 has been altered in some respects by Congressional review (the current projected expenditure is $422 billion), but, it is a valid benchmark of where DOD is headed in coming years.[2]

---

[2] Office of the Under Secretary of Defense (Comptroller), *National Defense Budget Estimates for FY2005* (Washington, DC: Department of Defense, 2004). Six DOD-issued documents also used in this study include: *Financial Summary Tables, Procurement Programs, Operations Programs, Construction Programs, RDT&E Programs*, and *Program Acquisition Costs by Weapon Systems*. All were issued in early 2004. See Jonathan Weisman and Thomas Ricks, "Increase in War Funding Sought", *Washington Post*, October 26, 2004, A1, for details on the planned supplemental for fiscal year 2005.

Table 1. Recent Trends in Defense Budgets (Budget Authority in Current $Billions)

	2003	2004	2005	2006	2007	2008	2009
Budget Request and Forecast, Feb. 2002	378.6	387.4	408.3	492.2	450.9		
Budget Request and Forecast, Feb. 2003		379.6	399.6	419.6	440.4	461.7	
Budget Request and Forecast, Feb. 2004			402.6	423.6	444.9	466.7	488.9

Actual Budgets after Wartime Supplemental Appropriations and Other Changes
                437.8   441.7   Not Available

Recent supplemental appropriations thus have elevated defense budgets well above the levels originally requested by DOD for its basic budget. While these supplemental appropriations have paid for wartime operations, they have not enlarged the funds available for normal peacetime measures or allowed DOD to pursue transformation faster. Only time will tell how large future supplementals might be, or whether supplementals will continue to be the prevailing practice. Regardless of what the future holds, the key point is that unless direct wartime costs as well as their indirect ripple effects are specially funded, the basic budget will have to be drawn upon in ways that draw money away from other accounts, including procurement.

Table 2 shows how the defense budget has been changing not only in current dollars, but in constant dollars as well—for both BA and outlays. BA spending rose by 2.2 percent annually during 1998-2000. During 2000-2002, it rose by an annual average of 6.25 percent. From 2002-2005, excluding supplemental appropriations, the average annual increase would be 2.95 percent. During 2005-2009, defense spending excluding supplementals is projected to rise 2.5 percent annually. If so, the effect will be to slow down the rate at which real defense spending is increasing each year. Beyond 2009, the best estimate is that DOD budget may increase in current dollars to offset inflation, but constant dollar expenditures will remain at about the 2009 level. Thus, the real increases of 2005-2009 will elevate the defense budget onto a higher plateau, but after that, the budget could remain on this plateau even though pressures for greater spending may be mounting.

Table 2. Trends in Current and Constant Dollars
(Budget Authority and Outlays in $Billions)

		1998	2000	2002	2005	2007	2009
Budget Authority	*Current Dollars*	258.6	290.5	345.6	402.6	444.9	488.9
	Constant 2004 Dollars	308.0	328.8	369.9	402.6	424.1	443.0
Outlays	*Current Dollars*	256.1	281.2	332.1	429.6	426.9	467.9
	Constant 2004 Dollars	304.3	318.5	354.7	429.6	407.4	424.5

Table 3 provides a perspective on the size of today's defense budget, which includes funds for DOD and foreign intelligence, by comparing the trends of today to those over the past 45 years. In constant 2005 dollars, defense budgets since 1960 have ranged from about $300 billion to $480 billion in response to shifting requirements, and have averaged $365 billion. The 2005 budget request of $402.6 billion is 10 percent above average, but it is still less than the peak Reagan years and consumes a smaller share of the federal budget and gross domestic product (GDP) than was the case in the distant past.

Table 3. Historical Trends in Defense Spending (in $Billions)

	Current $	Constant $	% Federal Budget	% GDP
1960	40.9	314.8	45.0	8.0
1965	49.1	340.0	38.8	6.7
1970	74.1	394.2	39.4	7.6
1975	85.7	305.7	25.5	5.4
1980	142.6	330.7	22.5	4.9
1985	286.8	480.7	25.9	5.9
1990	293.0	423.3	23.1	5.1
1995	255.7	326.5	17.2	3.6
2000	290.5	328.8	15.7	2.9
2005	402.6	402.6	17.9	3.6

Students of today's defense budgets often note that the United States is spending more than its allies in Europe and Asia, who spend only about $225 billion on military preparedness each year ($150 billion in Europe, the remainder in Asia). Although critics imply that the United States is spending too much on its military forces, it can be argued that several allies are spending too little and their forces are not prepared for new-era missions. Many allies have small military budgets because of the security provided by the United States, without which their defense budgets often would have to double in size. In addition, the United States faces military requirements that are more demanding than those faced by most allies, who largely are dealing with their own regions, not the entire world. Owing to its global responsibilities, the United States must have a multifaceted military of command, control communications, computers, intelligence, surveillance, and reconnaissance (C4ISR), as well as space systems, nuclear forces, mobility forces, ground forces, air forces, naval forces, special operations forces, logistic support forces, and other assets, all of which must be modern, sustainable, and ready. These forces must be able to project power to remote regions and be capable of handling multiple crises. Inevitably a large defense budget will continue to be needed to meet these requirements, even if key allies can be motivated to perform better.

As the U.S. military carries out global missions, it faces another reality: the cost of defense continues to rise. Such cost increases are a natural consequence of growing productivity that yields benefits in enhanced military strength. By a wide margin, today's U.S. military fields qualitatively better forces than decades ago. But the price of these improvements has steadily elevated budgets. As shown in table 4, the annual cost per active-duty soldier has more than doubled in constant dollars since 1960, and today totals $272,949. The jump in recent years is noticeable, but the upward trend has been evident for decades. Over the past 15 years, per-capita defense costs have risen at about 2-3 percent annually even though procurement expenses were unusually low. In the future, these trends could compel DOD to make painful cuts in force structure or investment programs.

Table 4. Trends in Costs of Defense Business

	Budget: Constant 2005 $ Billions	Active Military Manpower (000's)	Cost per Active Serviceman
1960	314.80	2,476.00	$127,140.00
1970	394.20	3,066.00	$128,571.00
1980	330.70	2,063.00	$160,300.00
1990	423.30	2,144.00	$197,434.00
2000	328.80	1,449.00	$226,915.00
2005	402.60	1,475.00	$272,949.00

What accounts for these per-capita cost increases? One reason is that the size of the military has shrunk, while defense spending has fluctuated. A second reason is that military salaries and benefits have become more competitive since the end of conscription; competitive compensation is needed to recruit and retain high-quality people. Third, the cost of new weapons has risen at a relatively high rate; modern fighters, ships, and tanks cost more than before, and they perform better. Fourth, costs for military operations have risen due to the expense of modern fuels, materials, spare parts, supplies, and buildings. Finally, today's military must operate at a faster tempo.

Given the current world situation, the defense budget likely will need to continue growing in future years to offset inflation and provide real growth. What should be avoided is a repetition of past feast-and-famine cycles. Such cycles prevent defense funds from being wisely invested in good times or bad. Although some projections envision no real growth after 2010, they ignore the coming procurement agenda and other pressures for higher spending. If real increases of 2-3 percent were appropriated annually, the defense budget would continue to consume a constant share of GDP, assuming the national economy grows at the same rate.

Given the national trends facing the federal budget in the decade ahead and the levels of defense spending predicted by CBO beyond 2009, the target of 2-3 percent real growth in the defense budget may not be met. It is in the context of this tighter long-term budget that we examine six key defense-spending issues.

The challenge is to craft new spending practices for a period of projected budgetary constraints. Affordability and performance will need to be the governing criteria for all programs. Knowing this, DOD is shifting emphasis away from viewing strategy and transformation in theoretical terms and toward seeing budgets and costs as key factors. Six key strategic issues merit special attention because they will have a large

5

bearing on how defense spending and U.S. military preparedness unfold in the next decade. They are:

1. Pursuing transformation: joint expeditionary warfare and long-term dominance
2. Strengthening the Army: more investment funds and new capabilities
3. Forging new program priorities: reducing support costs to create savings
4. Balancing DOD line-item budgets: controlling O&M spending
5. Guiding RDT&E: more basic research, faster production, cost control
6. Shaping procurement: the challenge of investing scarce funds wisely.

Issue One: Two Transformation Goals

Strengthening U.S. forces for waging expeditionary warfare along the southern arc of instability—the large zone from the Balkans to South Asia, including the Greater Middle East—while also transforming for new operations will be main endeavors for defense strategy and budgets. These two transformation goals are strategic partners, not mutually exclusive. Pursuing both goals at the same time, however, may be challenging because of the looming budget constraints discussed above. In some respects, the capabilities and investments needed for near-term expeditionary operations are different from those needed for long-term transformation. DOD will need to strike a sensible balance between these two goals and extract savings from elsewhere in the defense budget to fund them. DOD is well aware of the need to balance risks and priorities; the issue is how best to do so in an era of shifting strategic requirements.[3]

	Near Term Preparedness for Expeditionary Warfare	**Long-Term Transformation for Strategic Dominance**
Key Priorities	Joint Operations with Massed "Boots on Ground" Stabilization Operations	High-Tech, Stand-off Strike Net Centric Capabilities Naval and Air Platforms

Transformation is a protracted process of making major changes in technology, structures, operations, business practices, and culture to prepare U.S. forces for 21st century warfare. As conceived before September 11 2001 and the beginning of the GWOT, the main purpose of transformation was to prepare U.S. military forces to enhance strategic dominance over potential adversaries in the long-term. Threats were considered to be medium-size rogue powers and large, near peer rivals, such as China. While generic in principle, one of the key agendas has been to create high-tech standoff strike forces aided by information networks, sensors, and smart munitions that can play lead roles in combat. This approach to transformation relies heavily on air power, naval power, and related joint assets to win wars. It de-emphasizes the traditional roles of massed ground forces, calling instead for dispersed ground forces to perform missions that air strikes can't accomplish. This approach also calls for ground forces that rely on indirect, standoff fires from attack helicopters, missiles and rockets, or other artillery rather than close combat units of tanks and infantry.

By contrast to long-term transformation goals and plans, the expeditionary wars waged as part of the GWOT have required different types of transformed joint forces. Such wars necessitate boots-on-the-ground assets for many new missions that require large ground forces for close-in fighting and for performance of demanding stabilization and reconstruction (S&R) operations. These missions often do not place major emphasis

---

[3] Office of Force Transformation, *Military Transformation: A Strategic Approach* (Washington, DC: Department of Defense, 2003). See also the transformation roadmaps issued by the military services.

on air strikes across the entire spectrum of operations. This type of war requires more than merely dislocating and defeating enemy maneuver units on the battlefield; U.S forces also must suppress enemy forces that, after losing on the battlefield, retreat into cities, mountains, and forests to conduct guerilla warfare. S&R further requires establishing new governments to rule countries occupied by U.S. forces. Ultimately, the military is being tasked not only to win the war, but also to help win the peace locally. These missions are carried out by ground forces operating in complex situations quite different from those envisioned in standoff-strike theory.

Preparing for joint expeditionary wars is not solely the province of ground forces. It also requires reconfiguring air and naval assets. Air forces must be prepared to provide precision air-to-ground fires that can be integrated closely with ground fires and maneuvers to dislocate and destroy enemy ground combat forces. An example is the integrated air-ground fires and maneuvers that took place during the advance on Baghdad in Operation *Iraqi Freedom* (OIF). Likewise, naval forces must be configured for expeditionary and littoral missions of the sort that took place during operations in Afghanistan and Iraq. Both the Navy and U.S. Air Force (USAF) have been taking major steps to meet these new requirements, yet additional changes may be necessary as new priorities emerge for operations, information networks, forces, weapons, munitions, and support assets.

The key point is that future expeditionary missions will continue to demand unique joint approaches to force design and operations. Moreover, the force posture best suited to expeditionary missions in the near-to-mid term may be different from the posture needed to deal with China or a similar adversary in the long term. A challenge facing defense planning will be to field forces that can perform expeditionary missions while providing the adaptability to shift to new threats and different missions over the horizon. To be sure, some joint forces and information systems can operate effectively in domains of both expeditionary conflicts and future warfare, but this is not true across the entire posture because not all forces are highly flexible. For example, aircraft carriers and fighter wings cannot provide boots on the ground, and infantry divisions cannot perform deep strike missions. Likewise, current ground combat forces are not suited to many S&R missions. The solution to this problem is not to pursue either expeditionary missions or future transformation at the expense of the other, but to strike a sensible and evolving balance between them. Doing so, however, requires careful analysis of how to allocate future budgets and manpower and how to reconfigure U.S. forces.

The Initial DOD Approach to Transformation

For most of 2001, when the most recent *Quadrennial Defense Review (QDR)* was being written, DOD focused on crafting a new defense strategy and accelerating transformation, which had begun in the late 1990s. The strategy of preparing to fight two major theater wars (MTW's) was replaced by a capability-based strategy anchored in a "1-4-2-1" concept for sizing the force, as illustrated below. This concept held that versatile U.S. military forces should provide homeland defense and be capable of operating in four geographic regions in situations short of major war. It also mandated that U.S. forces must be prepared for two concurrent major wars, including one war that could require occupation of an enemy country.[4]

1-4-2-1 Strategic Concept

1—Homeland defense
4—Normal defense operations in four key regions
2—Two nearly concurrent major combat operations
1—Occupation of a conquered country

Since then, DOD and the rest of the U.S. government have been implementing the new strategy. Considerable progress has been made in building better homeland defense capabilities, including the creation of a Department of Homeland Security, but much work remains. The Pentagon still resists accepting a significant role in Homeland Security. To handle the four key regions where U.S. military commands are focused, DOD has been developing a new, long-term plan for global overseas presence that will reduce peacetime troop deployments by 60,000-70,000 (235,000 are deployed now) while also creating new assets—for example, increased prepositioning of equipment and new operating facilities—to enhance U.S. military responsiveness. The greatest focus, of course, has been the waging of two regional wars in Afghanistan and Iraq, followed by two lengthy S&R missions after major combat operations had been completed. The 1-4-2-1 concept is already stressed. Whether it will remain valid for the coming years remains to be seen, but the key point is that in 2001, the concept provided a new strategic framework for guiding transformation.

The *QDR* instructed that transformation should focus on six goals that called for improvements in 1) missile defenses and other homeland security, 2) information networks, 3) information security, 4) space assets, 5) swift power projection, and 6) standoff strike forces capable of denying sanctuary to enemies. It is noteworthy that these six goals said little about close combat, much less such boots-on-the-ground missions as attacking terrorist cells, stabilization, or reconstruction. In the eyes of some observers, these six goals were animated by a desire not only to gird for regional wars and similar near-term conflicts, but also to prepare for a military confrontation with China or some other peer rival in 10-20 years. This emphasis on high-tech strike forces for major combat operations was endorsed publicly by the Joint Chiefs of Staff (JCS) in *Joint Vision*, which presented a concept of joint operational warfare for full-spectrum missions plus such additional warfighting concepts as information networking, dominant maneuver, precision engagement, focused logistics, and full-dimension protection.[5] While it said little about the exact mix of forces, its concepts envisioned a balanced combination of assets from all services. Mutually reinforcing concepts tabled by the services—network-centric warfare, rapid decisive operations, and effects-based operations—reinforced the *Joint Vision* focus on major combat operations by high-tech strike forces as well as ground forces prepared for intense combat.

---

[4] Office of the Secretary of Defense, *Quadrennial Defense Review Report 2001* (Washington, DC: Department of Defense, 2001).
[5] Chairman, Joint Chiefs of Staff, *Joint Vision* (Washington, DC: Department of Defense, 2002). See also accompanying Joint Staff studies of joint operations concepts.

These new-era concepts emphasized joint operations not only because they made sense in theory, but also because they were made possible by the end of the Cold War. During the Cold War, U.S. ground, air, and naval forces had mostly operated in separate domains to defeat distinct, sizable threats. Afterward, the disappearance of the Soviet adversary eliminated the prospect of major enemy air and sea threats. This development enabled the U.S. military to forge its potent ground, air, and naval assets into a joint force that could wage land warfare by all three components collaborating together. Whereas ground forces provided about 80 percent of firepower for land warfare during the Cold War, new-era joint operations envisioned about 50 percent of firepower coming from ground forces, with the remaining 50 percent coming from air-delivered strikes, including such standoff assets as bombers and cruise missiles. The pinpoint accuracy and lethality of smart munitions facilitated this enhanced reliance on air-delivered strikes.

As a consequence, this joint doctrine implied that fewer ground forces could be employed in each operation, provided that sufficient air and naval forces were present to make up the difference. The effect was to reinforce the rationale for a balanced force posture of 10 active Army divisions, 3 Marine Expeditionary Forces (MEFs), 10 USAF Air Expeditionary Forces (AEFs) with 20 fighter wings, and 12 Navy carrier strike groups. Transformation called for a long-term effort aimed at equipping this posture with advanced information networks, sensors, munitions, and new-era platforms to carry out this vision of joint warfare. As of now, programs totaling $239 billion for 2005-2009 are officially listed as transformational. Table 5 displays how funds are allocated among key transformation goals. Other modernization and investment programs also contribute importantly to preparedness goals. The Air Force and the Navy are both entering a lengthy modernization effort to procure new combat aircraft and warships. This effort will accelerate after 2010 and continue through 2020. Its high costs will create a procurement bow wave that places additional strains on future defense budgets, but it will support transformation and strengthen U.S. combat power.

Table 5. DOD Transformation Budget (BA in $Billions)

Transformation Goals	Funding for 2005	Funding Thru 2009
Defend U.S Homeland and Overseas Bases	7.90	55.00
Project and Sustain Forces in Distant Theaters	8.00	96.00
Deny Enemies Sanctuary	5.20	49.00
Improve Space Access and Capabilities	0.30	5.00
Improve and Protect Information Networks	2.90	34.00
Total	24.30	239.00

The Impact of Expeditionary Wars

The transformation plan launched by DOD was barely underway when September 11, 2001 changed the strategic equation facing the U.S. military. Initially the war on terrorism confirmed DOD emphasis on high-tech warfare that blended major air-delivered strike operations with limited numbers of ground forces. The war in Afghanistan was won mainly by air strikes directed by spotters on the ground and few ground combat forces. Brigade-sized operations began only in March 2002, toward the end of the effort to topple the Taliban and disrupt al Qaeda. The invasion of Iraq in early 2003 was carried out by a combination of air strikes and a ground posture of only 5 1/3 U.S. and British divisions, fewer ground forces than had been thought necessary for a Persian Gulf war. The occupations of Afghanistan and Iraq, however, have shed different light on new-era expeditionary operations and their requirements. Today, fully 130,000 U.S. ground troops occupy Iraq and about 15,000 remain stationed in Afghanistan. The effect of these enduring commitments has been to strain not only active Army and Marine forces, but Reserve Component (RC) forces as well. Meanwhile, U.S. air and naval forces have been partly relegated to the sidelines, often unable to make major contributions to irregular combat operations that must be performed almost exclusively by ground forces performing wartime occupation duties.

The occupations of Iraq and Afghanistan, coupled with the U.S. presence in the Balkans and numerous Special Operations Forces (SOF) missions, make clear that the GWOT will require more boots on the ground than was envisioned earlier. It will require ground forces that can perform not only major combat operations, but also S&R missions. In addition to mandating parallel changes to air and naval forces, it also will require investments in such assets as a new global overseas presence, so-called "low density/high demand" (LDHD) forces, SOF forces, bases and facilities, military commands, information networks, prepositioned equipment, strategic lift, and funds for training with new partners. Such a family of measures especially will be needed if the vast "southern arc of instability" from the Balkans to the East Asian littoral remains a hotbed of instability, terrorism, and other dangerous threats that could mandate regular U.S. military interventions. Such changes cannot be made quickly, but they can be done over the mid-term in 3-8 years. Becoming better prepared for expeditionary wars and other GWOT missions thus has become an important goal of defense transformation.

In response to the need for more ground forces, DOD is enlarging the Army by about 30,000 active troops at least temporarily, is restructuring active brigades to increase their number from 33 to 43-48, and is rebalancing the active and reserve forces to increase the supply of units capable of occupation duty. In the eyes of some, this limited force expansion and reconfiguration is based on the premise that the occupation of Iraq is a spike. If such demanding expeditionary missions continue, a permanent expansion could be needed, and its size is uncertain. Some observers have suggested enlarging the active Army from 10 divisions to 12, the size of the base force in the early 1990s. Adding more active manpower, rather than reorganizing current manpower to add two divisions could require up to 100,000 additional troops. Such a force expansion would be expensive; the annual cost could be $15-20 billion for manpower, training, equipment, and stocks. The addition of 40,000-50,000 troops would cost less, but again, would not be cheap.

Finding the Money for Expansion

Assuming a modest increase of Army manpower, costs for a solid program of this and other measures could be about $15-20 billion per year. What would be the source of these funds? Perhaps economizing across the board can generate sufficient savings. If this solution is not pursued, the inevitable source will be DOD acquisition programs. A reallocation of $20 billion away from the procurement and RDT&E budgets would constitute a 12-14 percent cut. The impact on modernization and transformation could be disproportionately greater because new weapons and technologies will be likelier candidates for termination than basic infrastructure, secondary items, and supplies. A permanent enlargement of the Army may make sense, but its size should be considered carefully, with the benefits, costs, and tradeoffs in mind. While the Army needs more deployable forces, first priority should go to making better use of manpower now assigned to domestic, non-deployable functions—nearly 40 percent of the total. If a too-expensive enlargement is pursued, the Army's own modernization programs, already under-funded, could become victims.

If cuts in transformation programs are required, a strong case can be made that U.S. defense strategy should place a shifting, phased emphasis on the twin goals of preparing for boots-on-the-ground missions and related expeditionary operations as a key transformation goal in the near-mid term, and pursuing in a phased way the high-tech transformation for standoff strike operations and possible competition with a peer rival in the long term. Three years ago, DOD emphasized the latter at the expense of the former. The strategy put forth here avoids the mistake of pursuing the former at the unwise expense of the latter. It also elevates preparedness for expeditionary warfare to a high and enduring position in U.S. defense planning, while allowing for priorities between these two goals to be adjusted over the passage of time.

This strategy of focusing currently on preparing for expeditionary wars while still investing in strategic dominance as a hedge has implications for how future defense budgets are spent. For DOD, the coming imperative will be to find a sensible balance between the two goals so that both arenas are adequately funded. Preparedness for expeditionary warfare may need to be given elevated priority in the near-mid term, but in the long term, it is likely that expeditionary warfare will decline in priority and high-tech transformation for strategic dominance will deserve growing attention. Sequencing funding for these two goals will be critical.

Issue Two: Strengthening the Army

Enhancing the preparedness of U.S. forces for expeditionary warfare can be seen as a variant of the high-tech transformation that has been pursued since 2001. It will require unique programmatic measures that will need to muscle their way into a defense budget not currently designed to fund them. Strengthening the Army's capacity to put the right forces in the right places at the right times is the heart and soul of becoming better prepared for expeditionary missions. In addition to adding manpower, what else can be done to help the Army? Recently the Army has been responding to outside advice by shifting emphasis toward near-term preparedness at the expense of transformation. Even so, some critics portray the Army as not being at the forefront of successful innovations. Such critics point to cancellation of the Crusader artillery tube and the Comanche attack helicopter (a step proposed by the Army) and other controversies. Their criticisms underscore the need to craft measures that not only make sense to the Army, but also gain traction across DOD.

Under Investment

One reason why the Army has innovated slowly in recent years is that it has lacked sufficient investment funds to develop and procure new weapons systems. Although cancellation of the Crusader and the Comanche may have freed funds for other programs, the Army thus far has had trouble funding many investment programs for its current forces. Table 6 shows that in the current Future Year Defense Program (FYDP) the Army will have only $120.4 billion for RDT&E and procurement during 2005-2009. This amount is far less than the $265.4 billion and $293.2 billion available to the Navy and Air Force, respectively. This difference stems from larger Navy and USAF budgets and from the ability of both services to spend more of their budgets on investment than does the Army.

Table 6. Service Investment Budgets: 2005-2009 (BA in Current $Billions)

	Procurement	RDT&E	Total Investment	Total Spending	Percent Spent on Investment
Army	71.1	49.3	120.4	535.4	22
Navy	189.0	76.4	265.4	660.0	40
USAF	183.0	110.5	293.5	662.2	44

This disparity is nothing new. As table 7 demonstrates, the Air Force and Navy have had bigger investment budgets than the Army for decades. Several reasons help explain the disparity. The Navy and Air Force are more capital-intensive than the Army; ships and aircraft cost more to acquire than tanks and artillery tubes. The Navy and Air Force also participate in expensive, high-technology programs, such as nuclear forces and space, that do not involve the Army in major ways. Because the Navy and Air Force have larger total budgets and face lower expenses in other areas like personnel and O&M, they are able to free more funds for acquisition. The Army does not need investment budgets as big as those of the Navy and USAF. But it does require enough funds for RDT&E and procurement to pursue its own weighty requirements.

Table 7. Trends in Investment Budgets (BA in Current $Billions)

	1975	1985	1995	2005	2009
Army	4.00	23.70	11.90	20.80	26.80
Navy	11.20	43.20	25.80	44.00	62.30
USAF	9.20	55.20	28.30	53.70	63.70

For 2005, the Army's $20.8 billion investment budget is divided evenly into RDT&E and procurement. Its $10.4 billion procurement budget is only about one-third those of the Navy ($27.7 billion) and USAF ($32.6 billion). Because the Army is compelled to spend $4.7 billion on such secondary items as trucks, support equipment, and spares, it is able to allocate only $5.7 billion for procurement of such major items as aircraft and ground weapons, missiles, and electronics and communications equipment. It is spending only $1.6 billion to improve its ground weapons. This includes $905 million for procuring Stryker light combat vehicles—the only new major weapon being bought— and $400 million for modifying Abrams tanks and Bradley Infantry Fighting Vehicles (IFVs). By contrast, the Navy is spending $9.9 billion on shipbuilding and conversion, plus $8.8 billion on procuring or modifying combat aircraft. The Air Force is spending $13.1 billion to acquire or modify combat aircraft and transports, $4.7 billion on missiles, and $1.7 billion on electronics and communications equipment. As a consequence, the Navy and USAF today are modernizing and transforming faster than the Army.

The Tradeoff: Present Needs versus Future Capabilities

Recently the Army has been reacting by trimming its investments in Future Combat Systems (FCS) to increase spending on upgrades for current forces. While this prioritization makes sense, it underscores the dilemmas facing Army investment spending. During 2005-2009, the Army will benefit from growing DOD budgets for investment, but it will continue receiving only its current 18 percent share of the total. Its investment budget for 2009 will be only $6 billion larger than now. By comparison, the Navy will receive $18 billion more; the Air Force $10 billion more. Thus, the current disparity between the Army and the other two services will continue to widen. An encouraging trend is that Army procurement funds are projected to grow to $18.8 billion in 2009. The additional funds will enable the Army to begin a long-delayed modernization program that could include initial FCS vehicles—if they are available by then—plus procurement or upgrades of other weapons. Nonetheless, the Army's procurement budget will trail the Navy's ($50.3 billion) and USAF's ($40.8 billion) by a wide margin, and this disparity will continue throughout the following decade as the other services accelerate modernization. At issue is whether the Army's smaller budgets for RDT&E and procurement will meet its legitimate needs in this era of GWOT and transformation. Provided the Army has attractive programs to fund, an increase of $3-5 billion per year could help greatly, though it would not alleviate all shortfalls. Such a step, of course, would require an effort to extract commensurate savings elsewhere in the DOD budget.

Even if the Army receives sufficient investment budgets, it will be able to contribute fully to expeditionary warfare only if it fields forces that are properly structured for this mission. To date, the Army's main innovation has been its six Stryker brigades, which will be equipped with light, wheeled armor. When FCS vehicles become available, they too will be lightweight. Some critics question whether Stryker and FCS vehicles will have sufficient cross-country mobility, firepower, and survivability. Many Abrams tanks and Bradley IFVs will be in the Army force posture for years because they have proven their mettle in both intense combat and demanding occupations. They should be upgraded regularly to keep them in top shape, not treated as legacy weapons doomed to extinction. If valid replacements for Crusader and Comanche can be found—such as networked artillery fires and an improved Apache attack helicopter—they should be priority candidates for procurement. For the foreseeable future, the Army will be best-served by retaining a robust mix of armored/mechanized, infantry, and airborne/air assault units rather than converting its entire posture to units armed with lightweight armor. Lightweight armor that is transportable by C-130 is fine, but it must be capable of winning battles once it arrives. Heavy armor can deploy fast enough for most crises if it is prepositioned or moved by fast sealift.

More and Smaller Brigades

A publicly announced plan calls for the Army's current active posture of 33 maneuver brigades to grow to 43-48 brigades, each of which could be made more independent by virtue of receiving attack helicopters, artillery, reconnaissance assets, and other equipment currently held at higher echelons. In maneuver units, the new brigades may be smaller than current brigades, containing, for example, two infantry battalions instead of three. The resulting posture will provide a robust mix of heavy, medium, and light brigades. The Army hopes to meet any additional manpower needs by trimming elsewhere in its force structure. The main benefit will be to give the Army more maneuver units to perform more missions, including rotational duties overseas. Critics worry that a smaller brigade will lack the firepower and sustainment needed for intense combat and other demanding missions. This tradeoff needs to be examined closely. The combination of smaller brigades and lightweight armor could result in insufficient combat power, thus producing brigades that, in relying heavily on standoff fires, can defend against serious opponents but not attack them. In the future, the Army will need not only a sufficient number of brigades, but also well-armed brigades capable of sustained offensive action.[6]

---

[6] As of this writing, the Army has not yet made decisions on how the deployment of additional brigades will be accompanied by changes in such command echelons as divisions, corps, and armies. Preliminary reports suggest that while the division and army echelons will be retained, the corps echelon will be

Equal in importance to reconfiguring Army combat forces is trimming the large logistic support structures and war reserves that accompany these forces and slow their deployment overseas. Deploying fewer and/or lighter combat vehicles will not appreciably speed deployment unless the Army's ponderous support assets are reduced. While progress toward leaner logistics has been made in recent years, support assets and stocks constitute about 600,000 of the one million tons needed to ship a heavy Army corps overseas. Trimming them seems possible because expeditionary combat often is less intense and enduring now than in the Cold War. If leaner support structures are fielded, combat forces can deploy faster—even if armed with heavy tanks—and will be less costly.

S&R Forces

A main Army shortfall needing remedial action is its lack of forces for S&R missions. Iraq has demonstrated that traditional ground forces can be hard-pressed to switch overnight from combat to S&R missions because they lack the necessary assets. S&R missions demand robust assets in such areas as military police, special operations forces, psychological operations, civil affairs, administration, civil engineers, public health, prison control, and others. Many of the required assets already exist in the Army, but they are not organized for S&R missions. The Army could create two division-sized S&R formations that possess the right assets along with sufficient combat forces to provide local security. One formation could be an active duty component and the other part of the RC posture.[7]

Two such formations, equipped with appropriate joint assets, would provide a sizable pool of modular, adaptable capabilities for use in multiple contingencies. Each would be organized into four brigades, capable of deploying in various sizes and combinations alongside combat forces so that they would be available to begin operations as major combat ebbs, not weeks or months afterward. In a contingency similar to the Iraq invasion, for example, the active division could deploy quickly to perform S&R missions as major combat operations are winding down. The RC division, in turn, could provide a rotational base for extended missions. If a bigger contingency arises, and the RC unit is activated, both divisions could deploy together. If multiple smaller contingencies arise, their brigades could be parceled out and distributed to combatant commands on an individual basis, thus providing wide coverage. For these reasons, a posture of two S&R divisions would provide the size and flexibility to cover most of the missions and risks ahead.

How could these S&R formations be manned? Fortunately, the Army's active and reserve postures already contain many of the relevant units assigned to corps and other high echelons. Many of the required units and manpower could be derived from reorganizing these units and focusing them on S&R missions. To the extent additional manpower is needed, the Army could trim manpower from domestic support agencies and fill remaining needs by enlarging is force structure. Reorganizing the Reserve

---

disestablished. In any event, the Army's main emphasis will be on establishing the brigade as its centerpiece unit for field operations.

[7] For more detail, see Hans Binnendijk and Stuart Johnson, *Transformation for Stabilization and Reconstruction Operations* (Washington, DC: Center for Technology and National Security Studies, 2003).

component will be easier because it possesses multiple formations that are not now needed for high priority combat units. Reorganizing the active Army will be harder, but perhaps some of the new combat brigades being created by the Army could be assigned to S&R formations to help provide the necessary combat power.

Strengthening Army preparedness for GWOT missions should be accompanied by upgrading the Marine Corps, which provides one-fourth of U.S. active ground forces. For 2005, the Marine Corps' procurement budget is only $1.4 billion, or 5 percent of total Navy procurement. This small budget is supposed to support a service that totals 175,000 active Marines and deploys three divisions and three air wings. On a per-capita basis, the Marine procurement budget is only about one-third that of the Army, which itself is low-funded. In the long term, the Marine Corps will benefit from acquisition of Osprey and Joint Strike Fighter (JSF), but an increase in its procurement budget could help upgrade current weapons, communications/electronics gear, missile and ammo stocks, and other assets. Like the Army, the Marine Corps needs to better organize its forces for S&R missions.

Issue Three: Reducing Support Costs to Create Savings

When new defense priorities must be pursued and tradeoffs accepted, attention often turns to the idea of reducing force structure in some areas to make room for more forces and investment programs in other areas. The idea of major force cuts, however, was rejected early in the Bush Administration for valid reasons. At the time, the Army was a candidate for reductions, but events since then point to the need for a bigger Army. A similar logic applies to air and naval forces. While some older aircraft and ships are being retired, the Air Force and the Navy are not over-endowed in relation to their global commitments, and developments could require their use in unanticipated ways. Beyond this, the general purpose forces consume only 36 percent of the defense budget. The other 64 percent should be considered as well. The best approach is to look not solely at force posture, but at the entire budget.

A good first step is to appraise funding trends for all 11 defense programs. As table 8 suggests, major changes in spending patterns have been underway in recent years. At issue is whether today's patterns should continue or altered to reflect new priorities. The budget share spent on general purpose forces may rise to about 40 percent by 2009, but this will leave about 60 percent of funds spent on other programs. One of the biggest is the program for intelligence and communications. Its growth since 1980 is significant; funded at $55.5 billion today, it will grow further by 2009. Another big program is training, medical, and other activities, which has shrunk since 1980 from 22.4 percent to 14.9 percent, but totals fully $60.1 billion today. Health care alone totals about $17 billion and is rising rapidly. Spending on R&D ($45.6 billion) and on Guard and Reserve Forces ($31.7 billion) falls into a third category of size. Spending on mobility forces at $20.8 billion and central supply and maintenance (CS&M) at $23.5 billion falls into a fourth category. The remaining programs are smaller. Table 8 shows how budget share for nuclear forces has dropped since the Cold War ended. It is projected to total about 2 percent of the budget through 2009, but spending on deployment of missile defenses—currently funded mostly by the R&D program—could elevate the percentage. A comparably small but also high-leverage program is SOF, which consumes less than 2 percent of the budget.

Table 8 illustrates why big savings cannot be achieved by taking a meat-axe to one or two programs. Such an approach can be devastating. For example, if $20 billion were extracted from a program of $65 billion, the program would lose fully 30 percent of its funds, a crippling portion. Focusing on a large number of programs and trimming each by a tolerable amount is a better way to economize. For example, if the goal is to increase spending on general purpose forces by $20 billion, the other 10 programs would need to be cut by about 8 percent each; a sizable portion, but not necessarily crippling. By spreading savings across multiple programs, the odds increase that defense preparedness will benefit from the transfer. In this example, a 14 percent increase for general purpose forces in exchange for 8 percent less to the other programs may be a worthy trade.

Table 8. Historical Trends in Distribution of Program Spending—TOA*

Percentage of DOD Budget

Programs	2005 (Current $Billions)	1980	1990	2000	2005
Strategic Forces	8.80	7.30	6.20	2.50	2.20
GPF Forces	144.00	36.80	38.60	36.80	35.80
Intel. and Comm.	55.50	6.10	9.90	11.10	13.80
Mobility	14.50	1.60	2.10	4.00	3.60
Guard/Reserve	31.70	6.30	6.40	8.50	7.90
R&D	45.60	7.40	8.70	9.20	11.30
CS&M	23.50	9.90	9.60	6.50	5.80
Tng., Med. and Other	60.10	22.40	14.80	16.70	14.90
Admin.	10.40	1.80	2.30	3.00	2.60
SOON**	1.40	0.04	0.03	0.03	0.03
SOF	7.10		1.00	1.40	1.80
Total	402.6	100%	100%	100%	100%

* *Author estimates based on 2004 data. DOD Green Book of March 2004 did not provide data for 2005*
***Support of Other Nations*

The Reserve Component and Support Programs

Some years ago, observers favored reducing Reserve component forces to save money. They targeted Army Guard and Reserve forces, whose 550,000 personnel allegedly contributed little to national security. This argument has been overthrown by the GWOT. Large numbers of Army Guard and Reserve forces have been called to active duty and have proven their worth in Iraq and elsewhere. The active Army depends on reservists to perform many combat support (CS) and combat service support (CSS) roles. In addition, reservists will have important roles in homeland security for many years. Arguably today's Army RC (Reserve and National Guard) combat posture of 8 divisions and 15 brigades is over-endowed, even as more CS/CSS troops are needed. Overall, recent events have shown that the RC posture is a bargain because it provides a large, usable manpower pool at modest expense. The RC budget is projected to grow from $31.7 billion in 2009 to about $40 billion in 2009; hardly a sign that contraction and savings are in the wind. Nonetheless, many reformers favor a rebalancing of RC assets, to focus on new-era missions and transition away from outdated ones.

Because of the growing premium on combat forces, the issue arises of whether five programs listed in table 9 that provide various types of support can absorb reductions to generate savings and investments on combat forces. Years ago, critics said DOD had too much tail and insufficient teeth. Since 1980, DOD has trimmed tail-heavy programs—CS&M; training, medical, and other activities; administration—from 34.1 percent of the budget to 23.3 percent. In recent years, base realignment and closing (BRAC) efforts have reduced basing costs. Even so, the support share of the defense budget grows to 48.5 percent when the programs for intelligence and communications and R&D are added to the ledger; the comparable figure stood at 47.6 percent in 1980. The main trend has been to transfer resources among these five support programs rather than reduce their total budget share.

Table 9. Trends in Support Programs*

Support Programs	2005 Budget ($Billions)	2009 Forecast
Intelligence and Communications	55.5	64.9
R&D	45.6	48.5
CS&M	23.5	25.8
Training, Medical, and Other	60.1	67.2
Administration	10.4	14.7
Total	195.1	221.1
Percent of Defense Budget	48.5	45.2

In 1980, these five programs consumed 47.6 percent of the DOD budget; in 1990, the figure was 45.3 percent

The reality is that, today, DOD spends fully $195 billion on these five support programs. In 2009, it may spend $221.1 billion; the biggest increases will take place in intelligence and communications and health care. Today, about one-half of active military manpower and most of it's the civilian workforce are employed in these programs. The result is that only about one-half of active servicemen—750,000 of the 1.4 million total—are available to deploy overseas in a war. Can these support programs be trimmed to generate savings in money and personnel? The argument against spending cuts is that many of these support activities are vital to the effectiveness of combat forces, which could not operate without satellites, information networks, well-maintained weapons, domestic infrastructure, and healthy, educated soldiers. Yet, nearly 50 percent of the budget seems a lot to spend on support programs when demands for combat forces and programs are mounting as budget constraints tighten. Only systematic analysis of details can determine whether and how these support programs might be trimmed or otherwise rebalanced. In the years ahead, they should be subjected to close scrutiny.

Issue Four: Controlling O&M Spending

Careful analysis also is needed of how funds are allocated among DOD's line-item budgets. Here too, new spending patterns may make sense to pursue new priorities. Table 10 displays expenditures and trends for the six functional categories. At first glance, historical continuity seems to be the rule, because each category has received a similar budget share for decades. But small shifts have taken place, and, over the course of years, such shifts can make a big difference in total funding for each category. The table offers rich insights into how the line-item budget has evolved over the years, how it may change, and how change will affect DOD ability to carry out accelerating procurement.

During the 1980s, DOD strategy called for a large force posture with a major emphasis on the purchase of new weapons. As a result, the categories of military personnel and procurement consumed 55 percent of the budget. During the 1990s, defense priorities changed. Reductions in force structure permitted less spending on military personnel. Because the DOD inventory was filled with new weapons, procurement spending shrunk. These two categories declined to 48 percent of the budget by 2000. Meanwhile spending on O&M rose to pay for accelerating daily operations of the forces, and spending on RDT&E rose to launch development of a new generation of weapons. During 2000-2005, new patterns began to emerge in response to rising O&M expenses—even as DOD strove to increase funding for RDT&E and procurement to accelerate transformation.

Table 10. Spending Patterns for Functional Activities (BA in Current $Billions)

Category	Expenditures		Trends (% Allocation)				
	2005	2009	1980	1990	2000	2005	2009
Military Personnel	106.3	122.1	30	27	28	26	25
O&M	141.2	164.6	32	30	39	35	34
Procurement	74.9	114	25	28	20	19	23
RDT&E	68.9	70.6	10	12	13	17	14
Construction and Housing	9.4	13.7	3	3	2	2	3
Other	1.9	3.9				1	1
Total	402.6	488.9	100	100	100	100	100

As table 10 shows, since 1990, spending on military personnel has declined slightly as a percentage of the defense budget, from 27 percent then to 26 percent now. This trend, however, conceals major shifts in the allocation of personnel funds. Since 1990, U.S. active military manpower has shrunk by about 30 percent. Meanwhile, per-capita pay compensation has been steadily rising to provide the competitive wages needed to sustain an all-volunteer force and to recruit skilled personnel in a growing domestic economy. During 2005-2009, military pay is forecasted to rise by about 15 percent in current dollars, but its share of the defense budget will decline to 25 percent because the budget is projected to rise somewhat faster. Other increases in total compensation, such as health care and housing, may be forthcoming in ways that indirectly increase spending on military personnel. In the near-term, military pay does not seem to be a barrier to pursuing transformation. After 2009, however, a problem could arise if the defense budget does not experience real growth. Military pay must grow in real terms to maintain competitive wages while other increases in compensation also must be funded. During 2010-2020, military pay and transformation thus could create conflicting priorities.

O&M Spending vs. Investments

In principle, spending on O&M is not an enemy of transformation. For example, the O&M budget helps fund joint training and professional military education, both of which contribute to transformation in important ways. Even so, the rising costs for today's O&M budgets are acting as a barrier to spending on RDT&E and procurement, which are the main engines of transformation. Expenses for O&M cover daily activities and must be paid regardless of the budget top-line. As a result, the funds available for investment (RDT&E and procurement) are a shifting variable. When defense budgets are falling, fewer funds can be spent on investment, but when budgets are rising, more funds can be spent. Because 1980 ended a budget drought, only 35 percent of the budget was spent on investment. During the Reagan buildup, the figure rose to about 40 percent, where it still stood in 1990. During the early 1990s, defense spending declined and DOD was on a procurement holiday because the weapons inherited from the Reagan buildup were still new and the Cold War was over. As a result, the percentage spent on investment fell to 30 percent by 1996 and stood at 33 percent in 2000. The budget increases since then have raised the share to 36 percent in 2005; it is expected to reach 37 percent by 2009. The main beneficiary will be procurement, which is expected to grow from $74.9 billion to $114 billion to fund the coming multi-service modernization program.

In recent years, the share allocated to O&M has risen in ways that have detracted from funds for investment. In 1980, as shown in table 11, investment spending roughly matched O&M spending. By 1985, with the Reagan buildup at full steam, investment spending exceeded O&M spending by 80 percent ($128.1 billion vs. $71.0 billion). Over the following decade, investment spending fell and O&M spending rose to the point that by 1995, the former was only 84 percent of the latter. Thereafter investment spending began rising again, but O&M also continued rising; during 1995-2005, the former rose by $65.6 billion, and the latter, by $47.4 billion. The result is that today, investment spending and O&M spending are about equal: $143.8 billion vs. $141.2 billion. During 2005-2009, investment spending is projected to rise to $184.6 billion with O&M spending growing to $164.8 billion. By 2009, investment spending is expected to exceed O&M spending by 12 percent, far less than the 80 percent margin of 1985. Over time, anticipated savings from BRAC will help constrain further growth of the O&M budget, but not enough to restore investment spending to its earlier pre-eminence over O&M.[8]

Table 11. Investment Budgets vs. O&M Budget (BA in Current $Billions)

	Spending (Procurement/RDT&E)	O&M Spending	Investment Spending (as a % of O&M Spending)
1980	48.8	46.4	105
1985	128.1	71	180
1990	117.8	88.3	133
1995	78.2	93.8	84
2000	93.7	108.8	86
2005	143.8	141.2	102
2009	184.6	164.6	112

Maintaining a large procurement budget is key to buying new weapons and other systems for expeditionary warfare and long-term transformation. If procurement spending of $114 billion is achieved in 2009, it will represent 23 percent of the DOD budget, the highest in many years, though still below the 33 percent sustained during much of the Reagan era, and lower than the 1990 figure of 28 percent at the end of the Cold War. Key issues arise about future procurement. Will a procurement budget of $114 billion in 2009 be enough to buy new-era weapons? What will happen afterward, when a procurement "bow wave"—multiple new weapon systems being bought at the same time—forms? Will procurement funds be adequate during 2010-2020? If more procurement funds are needed but bigger defense budgets are not available, can savings be found elsewhere in the defense budget?

These issues cast a bright spotlight on the O&M budget, not only because it is so large, but also because other line-item accounts are not attractive candidates for savings. Expenses for military personnel consume only 25 percent of the budget, a historical low, and nobody questions the importance of paying soldiers good salaries. The RDT&E budget currently is high at 17 percent of the total budget, but it is projected to decline to a more normal 14 percent by 2009. The budget for construction and housing is rising to update DOD buildings, create better military housing, and close bases, but by 2009, it will still hover at only 3 percent of the total budget. Can savings be found in the O&M budget? Equally important, can it be prevented from growing above future projections, thereby strangling the procurement budget? These two questions merit answers.

Today's O&M budget of $141.2 billion seems high when judged in proportion to other categories. Since 1997, non-war O&M had risen not only to reflect inflation, but also in real terms by about 3 percent per year. During 2005-2009, it is projected to grow from $141.2 to $164.6 billion, a $23.4 billion increase. This growth equates to a 4 percent annual increase, or about 1.5 percent annually in real terms. But if the non-war O&M

---

[8] BRAC results in increased construction costs in the near term and lowered O&M costs in the long term. For BRAC cost-savings to be fully realized, the entire program must be implemented.

budget grows at a rate of 5 percent annually—the rate experienced during 1995-2005—it could chop about $20 billion off acquisition spending in this period, and more thereafter. If DOD hopes to launch a major procurement effort later in this decade, it cannot afford to see the O&M budget continue to march steadily upward.

DOD is well aware of the tradeoffs posed by rising O&M budgets, and efforts are underway to control future growth. For example, the Navy is trying to squeeze O&M spending to generate more funds for procurement. Cutting O&M spending, however, is not easy. One powerful reason is concern for force readiness. Beyond this, O&M spending, including funds that do not contribute directly to readiness, is distributed among many dissimilar functional activities that are hard to analyze with regard to requirements, marginal productivity, and tradeoffs. DOD needs a management strategy for controlling the O&M budget to prevent unwarranted growth and, ideally, to create savings that can be channeled into procurement and other investments. Better analysis of this budget is imperative.

Reasons for O&M Growth

Of today's total O&M budget, about $50 billion is spent to pay the civilian workforce and the remainder is devoted to daily DOD functions. As table 12 demonstrates, the O&M budget is allocated among multiple categories. Roughly similar amounts are spent by the services and by DOD-wide agencies. Table 12 shows that the O&M budget is not synonymous with operations by active forces, which consume only $60 billion of the total. Within these forces, roughly $22 billion is spent on facility activities and restoration, and $5 billion is spent on depot maintenance. The amount actually spent on combat force operations thus is only $33 billion, or 24 percent of the entire O&M budget. Of the remaining $81 billion, $14.2 billion is spent on RC forces. DOD administration and service-wide activities such as logistic support consume fully $31.5 billion. The "Other" category of $20.5 billion includes DOD health care, which costs $17.6 billion for active personnel and retirees.

Table 12. DOD Request for Operations and Maintenance Budget 2005
(BA in Current $Billions)

	Army	Navy	USAF	DOD-wide	Total
Active Operating Forces	16.4	25.4	15.9	2.2	59.9
Mobilization / Mobility	0.5	0.8	3.3	0.1	4.7
Training and Recruiting	3.3	2.6	3.0	0.4	9.3
Administration & Service-Wide Activities	5.8	4.7	6.2	14.8	31.5
Guard and Reserve Forces	6.5	1.4	6.3		14.2
Other				20.5	20.5
Total	32.5	34.9	34.7	38.0	140.1

A noteworthy feature is how O&M spending per active-duty serviceman has increased over the past 30 years. Table 13 illustrates this trend by showing per-capita O&M costs in constant 2005 dollars since 1975. It shows an increase from $44,100 in 1975 to $97,720 today. Since 1975, O&M costs have risen by 220 percent in constant dollars. Moreover, the rate of increase has accelerated. During the 1970s and 1980s, per-capita spending rose by about 1.8 percent per year. From 1990-2000, it rose at 4.3 percent per year. Since 2000, it has been growing by 3.0 percent per year. Projections for 2005-2009 show an annual increase of only 1 percent, but this assumes that the 2009 O&M budget will grow to only $164.6 billion in current dollars or $148.1 billion in constant 2005 dollars.

Table 13. Trends in O&M Spending: Per-Capita Costs 1975-2005

	1975	**1980**	**1990**	**2000**	**2005**
O&M Budget (Current $Billions)	26.3	46.4	88.3	108.8	141.2
O&M Budget (Constant $Billions)	93.9	107.6	128	122.9	141.2
Military Manpower (000's)	2129	2063	2144	1455	1455
Per Capita Costs (Current $)	44100	52160	59700	84820	97040

Why has per capita O&M spending increased so much? Multiple reasons seemingly account for the upward trend. The cost of the civilian workforce, however, is not one of the reasons. Since 1980, this cost (in constant 2005 dollars) has shrunk from $60 billion to $50 billion; reductions in the civilian workforce from 991,000 to 688,000 people have offset the cumulative impact of real pay increases. Nor do training and exercises by the active forces provide a major reason. As previously mentioned, these forces consume only 24 percent of the O&M budget, and their training regimens remain similar to past years. The rising tempo of non-wartime international activities is one source of increase. In other areas, the rising operational and personnel tempo of the U.S. military doubtless has played a contributing role, but public data do not exist on the exact impact.

Elsewhere O&M costs have risen for well-known reasons. Soaring health care costs, including for retirees, are a strong reason. DOD's sophisticated health care system, which must address both peacetime and wartime needs, is a contributing factor. Beyond this, rising costs reflect the explosion of health care expenses across the entire country as a result of an aging population and expensive medical technology. Further cost increases for health care seem inevitable in future years; CBO forecasts near doubling of health costs by 2022 (in real dollars). Similarly, in general, today's modern weapons cost more to maintain and repair than did their less-sophisticated predecessors. Moreover, these modern weapons were mostly bought in the 1980s and 1990s; their advancing age results in rising maintenance costs. Aging buildings and facilities also cost more to operate and maintain. The same applies to trucks and thousands of other vehicles, as well as to other equipment. Fuels, supplies, and spare parts also have experienced rising costs. About

$2.5 billion is paid for such expenses as environmental restoration, drug enforcement, and Former Soviet Union (FSU) threat reduction. DOD today is relying more heavily on private contractors, which normally are paid from the O&M budget. Underlying these and other specific factors is another phenomenon: O&M money is popular within DOD because it can be spent quickly, yields prompt results, and is not subjected to the stringent cost controls of manpower and procurement budgets.

Today, there is no strategic theory to define O&M requirements, no lid to keep a tight ceiling on the O&M budget, and no strong sense of diminishing marginal returns; more O&M spending is almost always seen as better than less spending. O&M expenses rise because powerful constituencies support the rise and no potent barrier exists to stop it.

Many factors have interacted to push per-capita costs of O&M upward, but their exact contributions are hard to ascertain because adequate data do not exist to measure them. The attempt to determine future trends in O&M spending is beclouded by many uncertainties. In principle, if the operating tempo of U.S. forces remains high, O&M spending seems likely to remain high and could rise. Conversely, the continued introduction of new information systems may increase efficiency, thereby resulting in lowered O&M expenses. The retirement of older weapons as new weapons are procured may lessen O&M expenses—provided new weapons are not big O&M consumers.

Lamenting the lack of sufficient acquisition funds, an unnamed Pentagon official was reported by a newspaper to have said, "DOD is being eaten alive by O&M costs." If so, he was on target. Short of imposing an arbitrary spending ceiling, O&M is hard to control or manage from atop. It is a budget in which the devil lies in the details and at lower levels of the DOD bureaucracy.

Analysis of the O&M budget determinants and identification of high-leverage strategies for reducing O&M spending are needed. Better mastery of its many components and determinants is key to tempering O&M spending while ensuring that funds are allocated properly among its many parts. In recent years, DOD has been developing an improved reporting system for monitoring readiness. But O&M expenses involve many activities that extend beyond the traditional domain of combat readiness. The situation requires development of improved metrics, including measures of effectiveness, criteria of evaluation, and performance curves, for assessing the O&M budget as a whole.

Issue Five: More Basic Research, Faster Production, Cost Control

Transformation is propelled in part by training, education, and organizational changes in the near term, but RDT&E and procurement are central to its prospects in the long term. Although DOD has been on a procurement holiday for years, its RDT&E budget has been reasonably high, averaging $43 billion per year since 1995 and rising to $68.9 billion for 2005. The result has been the fielding of new information systems, sensors, and munitions that have helped empower transformation and warfighting. In addition, the RDT&E process is now producing a new generation of fighters, warships, and ground vehicles that will be bought in the coming years, thereby fueling modernization and further transformation. Despite these successes, the RDT&E community faces challenges: articulating a strategic concept for RDT&E, increasing funds for basic research, speeding development of new weapons and technologies, and controlling expenses so that procurement budgets are not drained.

Table 14 displays the RDT&E budget that DOD requested for 2005. The first three categories include activities during early RDT&E, when research on new weapons and technologies is beginning. The final four categories cover the stages when new ideas have taken shape, prototypes are emerging, and new systems are being subjected to full-scale testing to determine whether they are ready for procurement. The difference between these two clusters is significant. The first three categories receive only 15 percent of the RDT&E budget; the final four receive 85 percent. The reason for spending most funds on the later stages is that a great deal of testing, evaluating, and further developing must occur after new weapons take physical shape and even after they are initially deployed. The early stages of creating them on drawing boards and assembling their technological components is critical, but less costly because it involves ideas, studies, and initial demonstrations rather than full-blown development and testing.

Table 14. Request for RDT&E Budget in 2005 (in Current $Billions)

Category	Funding
Basic Research	$1.3
Applied Research	$3.9
Advanced Technology Development	$5.3
Advanced Component Development and Prototypes	$15.3
System Development and Demonstration	$19.3
RDT&E Management Support	$3.3
Operational Systems Development	$20.5
Total	$68.9

One criticism leveled at the RDT&E budget is that it allegedly lacks a clear strategic concept regarding its specific aims and purposes. Critics charge that instead of serving a single clear vision of future U.S. force operations, it pursues many different visions without attaching priorities to them. The alleged result is an RDT&E effort for all seasons, one that aspires to elevate all components of the U.S. military in multiple ways. The counter argument is that because RDT&E is an experimental process aimed at defining the future, multi-pronged activities are not only necessary, but also desirable; a tightly focused RDT&E effort might neglect key forces or overlook new, unanticipated changes in military technology, thereby mortgaging the future. Thus far, this debate has been resolved by vigorously pursuing technologies that seem likely to produce high-leverage payoffs while also casting a wide net for new, unanticipated technologies. While this approach may maximize the scope and wide-ranging productivity of the RDT&E effort, it seems likely to ensure that in the coming era of rapid technological change, RDT&E spending will remain high. Perhaps the RDT&E budget will not grow in future years, but it seems unlikely to shrink in ways that provide major savings. If a valid strategic concept can be created, it could help DOD channel RDT&E spending in focused directions without neglecting important areas of technological development.

Critics also question whether enough funds are allocated to basic scientific research in the first stage of the RDT&E cycle. Such research has made many seminal contributions to U.S. defense preparedness; radar in World War II and stealth technology in the 1980s are classic examples. A DOD goal has been to set aside 3 percent of the RDT&E budget for such research, but for 2005, only about 2 percent was allocated (Congressional actions raised the amount). Such research has a major impact on future weapons and technologies 10-20 years out. Such breakthroughs as information networks and smart munitions came from basic research, applied research, and advanced technology development, not from not testing of already assembled hardware. With today's small research budgets, less than $100 million is spent on in-house basic research by DOD laboratories. The remaining funds are contracted to outside sources, mainly universities. Outside research is necessary because most ideas for new technologies, especially information networks, are being developed there. Nonetheless, critics wonder whether DOD laboratories, which once were an engine of innovation, are being unwisely neglected. Shifting additional resources to basic research and funding of more in-house research might make sense and would not appreciably damage other RDT&E programs.

The services manage about $48 billion of the $68.9 billion total for RDT&E, and the rest is managed DOD-wide. Table 15 lists some of the biggest programs, which account for $32 billion of the total. Major funds are being invested into intelligence, communications, and space. The same is true for national missile defense. Together these two programs total about $23 billion, or one-third of the RDT&E budget. Major programs for new conventional weapons include the Joint Strike Fighter (JSF) (funded by USAF and Navy); FCS, the Army's armored combat vehicles; and the Navy's engineering of new ship designs. These three programs total $9 billion. The remaining $36 billion is spent to fund the roughly 800 additional programs in the RDT&E budget. Most of these programs focus on new technologies and weapons for the general purpose forces, but about $2 billion is spent on mobility forces, SOF, and logistic support systems.

Eventually many of these RDT&E programs will bear fruit. Even so, today's RDT&E process is not controversy-free. A big issue is whether it is capable of producing weapons quickly enough to meet modern requirements at affordable costs. In the past, RDT&E has been accused of taking too many years to field new weapons, of creating

Table 15. Major RDT&E Programs in 2005 (in Current $Billions)

Programs	Funding
Intelligence, Communications, and Space	$13.8
National Missile Defense	$9.1
F-35 Joint Strike Fighter	$4.6
Army Armored Combat Vehicles	$2.7
Navy Ship Engineering	$1.4

gold-plated weapons that cost too much to procure in adequate numbers, and of producing weapons that often fail to meet fresh requirements. The recent cancellation of Comanche, after years of expensive RDT&E, is evidence that this problem is not yet fully solved. During the 1990s, a typical acquisition program took 11 years to reach initial operational capability (IOC), a big increase from the 7-year cycle of the 1960s. DOD is now trying to reduce the average time to 8 years and, in the long term, ideally to 5 ½ years. Rather than waiting for completion of the full cycle, the emerging practice of spiral development aims to get new weapons into the force structure as quickly as possible, and to further develop them as operational experience is gained with them.

Employing RDT&E to propel transformation, while also controlling costs, will be a continuing challenge. Because transformation is an experimental process, it encourages an RDT&E effort that initiates, develops, and accepts or rejects many new designs, while modifying and improving them as they unfold. Transformation also encourages RDT&E programs that leap ahead into futurist technologies, and that equip major new weapons platforms with advanced performance characteristics. Examples of this emphasis on sophisticated technologies abound in the F-22, the FCS, and new ship designs. The problem with this technology-rich approach is that it can be expensive if fiscal control is lost. Today RDT&E for a major weapon can cost $10-20 billion or more. This reality, along with the practice of simultaneously funding hundreds of projects, has the effect of pushing RDT&E budgets upward.

In past decades, the RDT&E budget was only one-half or one-third the size of the procurement budget. Today's RDT&E budget is nearly as big as the procurement budget ($69 billion vs. $76 billion). By 2009, the procurement budget is projected to pull ahead ($114 billion to $76 billion), but this gain will occur only if the RDT&E budget does not rise above current projections. Recently, however, RDT&E costs for the JSF were increased significantly because of unanticipated problems and requirements. If increases of this magnitude are repeated regularly, they could drive the RDT&E budget upward and erode the procurement budget, thereby slowing modernization. Currently the RDT&E budget is projected to grow only by 2 percent during 2005 through 2009. If instead it grows by enough to offset inflation, it will rise to $76 billion and thereby reduce procurement spending by about $13 billion during 2005-2009 and more afterward. As DOD is aware, RDT&E budgets will need to be managed with cost control and economizing in mind.

Issue Six: Shaping Procurement

Coming years will witness the onset of a lengthy period of modernization in which large numbers of new weapons emerging from the RDT&E pipeline will be bought. This procurement effort, already underway, will gain momentum through 2009 and is scheduled to accelerate during 2010-2020 and afterward. The degree to which this effort can be fully accomplished will depend on the amount of procurement funds that are available over this period. Because funds may be tight, savings extracted from elsewhere in the defense budget could provide valuable additional resources for procurement. DOD could be hard-pressed to buy all of the new weapons in its plan on the desired schedule because sufficient funds may not be available to meet large requirements. If so, it will have to set priorities and make tradeoffs in shaping future procurement. The challenge is to make these tough decisions as wisely as possible.

At first glance, the projected increase in the procurement budget from $74.9 billion in 2005 to $114.0 billion in 2009 may seem adequate to solve the funding problem. Closer inspection, however, suggests a more-guarded conclusion. In constant 2005 dollars, today's procurement budget is only half of the average procurement budget of the Reagan years of 1981-1988, when the last modernization effort was launched. During these years, procurement rose from 27 percent of the budget in 1981 to 34 percent by 1983. Despite tapering to 28 percent in 1988, it averaged 32 percent for all eight years. The projected increase to $114 billion by 2009 will narrow the difference, but not close it. A principal impediment is the composition of the defense budget. Whereas the Reagan era witnessed 32 percent of defense budgets spent on procurement, today's share is 19 percent, and by 2009, the share will be 23 percent. Table 16 provides a frame of reference by comparing the projected 2009 budget to the distribution that would prevail if a hypothetical Reagan model (average Reagan-era expenses) still applied. It shows how the *combination* of higher spending on O&M and RDT&E drains funds away from procurement by up to $42 billion. While a return to the Reagan model is not possible owing to changes in defense affairs since then, DOD is paying a substantial opportunity cost for the growth in its O&M spending.

Table 16. Alternative Distributions of 2009 Defense Budget: Hypothetical Reagan-Era Model vs. Current Projection (in Current $Billions)

	Reagan-Era model	DOD Projection	Difference
Military Personnel	122.2	122.1	
O&M	136.9	164.6	+27.7
Procurement	156.4	114	-42.4
RDT&E	53.8	70.6	+16.8
Construction and Housing	14.7	13.7	-1.0
Other	4.9	3.9	+1.0
Total	488.9	488.9	

Because today's force posture is smaller than in the Reagan era, arguably a procurement budget of only $114 billion for 2009 could provide proportional spending. But this calculus ignores the higher costs of today's weapons, which elevate the spending requirement upward by $20-30 billion or more. Moreover, the 2009 projection of $114 billion is vulnerable to reductions in the defense budget and to unexpected rises in O&M and other accounts. Conversely, annual savings of $20 billion, by trimming the defense budget elsewhere, could elevate procurement spending by 18 percent. The impact on procurement of major weapons would be even larger. Because about $40 billion of the 2009 procurement budget must be spent on secondary items, only $74 billion will be available for major weapons. A $20 billion increase could elevate this spending by 27 percent, a substantial amount. If such savings are mainly invested in programs that do not require new weapons, however, modernization will need to unfold with currently planned procurement funds.

Regardless of future budgets, the coming modernization effort likely will not be carried out with the speed and vigor of the Reagan era. This applies not only to the coming four years, but also to the subsequent decade, when the procurement effort is intended to hit full stride because several new weapons from the Army, Navy, and Air Force will be emerging from RDT&E cycle at the same time, thus causing an upsurge of activity and expenses. During 2010-2020, procurement funds of about $1300 billion likely will be available if the defense budget is increased to offset inflation. Of this amount, about $845 billion will be available for new weapons; the remainder will be needed for steady-state procurement, including secondary items. As shown in table 17, an estimate is that spending requirements for new weapons in this period could total $775-$1,175 billion. If actual costs prove to be at the low end of this estimated range, future procurement budgets might be large enough to meet requirements. But if costs fall at the high end—a normal occurrence in the past—future procurement budgets could fall substantially short of requirements, thus compelling slower procurement than now envisioned. Funding shortfalls of 10-15 percent or more easily could occur. If so, DOD will need to make do with the funds actually available not only for the next five years, but for the coming 10-15 years as well. The procurement effort will need to be managed carefully during this entire period. Service plans cannot be merely stapled together without regard for their cumulative expense, and sacrifices and tradeoffs may be necessary in some areas.

Table 17. Future Procurement Budgets for New Weapons vs. Requirements 2010-2020, (in Current $Billions)

Forecasted Procurement Budgets	$845
Forecasted Spending Requirements	$775-1175
Potential Shortfall	$0-330

Spending requirements from 2005-2020 will be high not because of any single weapon, but because of the multiplicity of costly programs that must be funded in an across-the-board modernization. In addition to expeditionary warfare measures discussed earlier, current plans call for procurement of missile defenses, new ground combat vehicles, new fighters and other aircraft, and new ships. In the estimate shown in table 18, expeditionary warfare measures, such as S&R assets, revised overseas presence, and others, may cost $50-100 billion. Procurement of missile defenses might cost $75-150 billion or more depending, on the size of the posture being deployed. The Army's modernization and FCS program likely will cost $100 billion or more, but the exact amount is a variable owing to uncertainties about the Army's requirements, priorities, and budgets. The program for combat fighters and helicopters promises to cost about $300 billion or more. This program calls for procurement of about 4,000 new aircraft—a combination of F-22, F/A-18 E/F, F-35JSF, and F-45 Unmanned Combat Air Vehicles (UCAVs)—to replenish the aging inventories of the Air Force, Navy, and Marine Corps. In addition, the Marines will be acquiring the Osprey tilt-rotor helicopter and the Army likely will acquire more Apache helicopters to replace the cancelled Comanche. Of these air programs, the F-35 JSF is the most expensive; its 2,852 aircraft likely will cost $135-170 billion. Acquisition of expensive new support aircraft— mobility aircraft, tankers, C3 aircraft, and Anti-Submarine Warfare (ASW) aircraft—will add to the total for air modernization. Shipbuilding could also cost $300 billion or more. The Navy is planning to acquire new carriers and amphibious assault ships, the DD(X) destroyer and the CG(X) cruiser, the small Littoral Combat Ship (LCS), and Virginia-class attack submarines. The cost of the shipbuilding program especially will be high if the Navy pursues its goal of buying over 200 new ships and expanding its posture from 310 warships today to 376 ships in the distant future.[9]

---

[9] Although the new ground, air, and naval weapon systems will cost more than their predecessors, all are intended to bring major improvements in combat capabilities and to facilitate innovations in organizations and doctrines, thereby contributing importantly to transformation. For example, new ground weapons will be lighter and easier to deploy; new combat aircraft will bring a combination of stealth characteristics, better engines and avionics, and improved multi-mission performance; new ships will bring better hull design, propulsion systems, electronics, and weapons and smaller crews.

Table 18. Estimates of Future Procurement Programs and Costs 2005-2020 or Program Completion * (in Current $Billions)

Programs	*Potential Costs*
Expeditionary Warfare Measures	$50-100
National Missile Defense	$75-150
Army Modernization and FCS	$100-150
Combat Aircraft Modernization	$250-325
Support Aircraft	$50-100
Shipbuilding	$250-350
Total	$775-1175

* Author estimates based on multiple sources.

Critics deride many of these weapons as legacy platforms that are insufficiently transformational, but the reality is that virtually all provide major advances in technology and performance characteristics. They are key to strengthening U.S. military power in the coming years, and they facilitate transformation, not retard it. If better weapons can be found, they should be bought, but such futurist weapons are mainly on the drawing board, and their evolution will depend on experiences gained with the weapons about to be procured.

While all of these programs make military sense, how should DOD try to adjust if, taken together, the annual costs of these and other measures exceed the availability of procurement funds? Clearly, difficult choices and tradeoffs will have to be made. Some observers likely will call for cancellation of one or two big ticket programs in hope of solving the problem simply. Commonly cited candidates are the F-22 fighter and national missile defense, which already are targets of criticism. The drawback of this approach is that it could create gaping holes in the U.S. defense posture. Cancellation of the F-22 would save only about $40 billion because of the small number (280) being bought, and it would deprive USAF of the world's best fighter. Cancellation or a major truncating of the missile defense program could leave the United States vulnerable to enemy missile attacks. The same drawback applies to the idea of eliminating any other single procurement program; it would badly damage the capability of the U.S. military to carry out its future combat missions and pursue transformation. Entire programs should be terminated only if they truly can be spared in ways that do not leave the military bereft of critical capabilities and vulnerable to future threats.

In the eyes of many defense managers, the sensible solution in such situations typically has been to pursue an across-the-board approach that reduces funding of several programs in proportional ways. This approach is often characterized as unimaginative and unglamorous, but in strategic and economic terms, it can be the best way to ensure that a properly balanced posture emerges. The reason is that, while several programs may lose 10-15 percent of their resources, none are crippled and all are left with procurement efforts that, while not perfect, are acceptable. In essence, this approach strives to spread the risk in evenly distributed ways so that no programs and the forces relying on them are compelled to face unacceptable risks in the future.

This approach is not a solution for all circumstances; on some occasions cutting a few programs in big ways may make more sense then spreading reductions uniformly. An across-the-board solution does not necessarily mean that linear reductions should be imposed on all programs. Strategic decisions could yield a scheme of priorities in which some programs are reduced more than others. The key point is that, regardless of how programs are reduced individually, all of them still would receive sufficient funds to keep them viable and to maintain a sensible rate of production that responds to requirements faced. If this approach is adopted, it should come only after serious analysis of other options that includes cross-program tradeoffs and of implications for the defense industry. It should be embraced because it makes strategic sense, not because it is the path of least resistance.

Although most programs may be squeezed, the two programs that offer the largest potential savings are air modernization and shipbuilding, for the simple reason that they are the biggest, most expensive programs. Annual costs for air modernization can be reduced without crippling the enterprise by several stratagems: stretching out the procurement of new fighters and other aircraft, buying a high-low mix (for example, new-era F-16s), keeping older aircraft longer by rehabilitating them, buying fewer spare and replacement aircraft, reducing the size of fighter wings and squadrons, and resisting the temptation to make expensive product improvements as aircraft pass through the assembly lines. If necessary, lower procurement expenses can be pursued by adopting one of these stratagems or a family of them.

Naval shipbuilding is less susceptible to such stratagems because the number of weapons bought is smaller, construction of a ship can take years, and production schedules are harder to alter. The Navy's ambitious shipbuilding program reflects a strategic rationale, but it is vulnerable to budget shortfalls. For example, the 2005 plan to acquire seven new ships has been scaled back to four ships because of fiscal constraints. Critical choices may have to be made on the future size of the Navy and its force posture. A future Navy of 325-350 ships will cost less than one of 376 ships. A posture that includes numerous relatively cheap LCS ships will cost less than a posture composed of expensive surface combatants and attack submarines. The key issues to be addressed are: What kind of Navy will be needed in the future. How large should it be? How should it be configured? How should the Navy balance its need for expeditionary strike forces that can perform littoral missions with its enduring need for forces that can dominate the seas? These questions should be addressed in both strategic and economic terms, and decisions about the procurement budget should flow from the judgments made.

For air and naval forces, as well as other forces, such options for scaling back procurement goals and expenses are not painless. But together, they can enable procurement plans to be fitted to the funds available to them while ensuring that U.S. military forces are modernized at a rate fast enough to continue performing their missions. Ideally, the cuts will not be necessary if procurement costs for each weapon are kept under control, savings are extracted from elsewhere in the defense budget, and real budget increases are steadily funded. But because they could become a practical necessity, they need to be analyzed carefully so that a proper mix of them can be assembled and applied in a timely manner, and so DOD is not left clumsily trying to improvise at the last moment.

The Way Ahead

In summary, DOD faces the strategic challenge of determining how to pursue preparedness for expeditionary warfare in the near-to-mid term and high-tech transformation in the long term. Such preparedness may require a bigger and reorganized Army to provide more boots on the ground, but it also will require a host of other measures, such as new overseas facilities, prepositioned equipment, and operational practices. Long-term, high-tech transformation will require not only space systems, information networks, and smart munitions, but also procurement of many new weapons platforms by all services in the years ahead. Fully pursuing both goals will be difficult if, as seems likely, the defense buildup levels off and future budgets are not large enough to meet all plausible requirements. Since neither goal can be neglected, DOD will need to forge a budget strategy that achieves both goals to the highest degree possible not only in the next five years, but also in the coming 10-15 years.

Creating a Defense Budget Strategy and a National Security Budget

Although real spending increases after 2009 likely will be needed, DOD budget strategy will need to extract maximum strategic effectiveness from the funds that actually will be available. Performing this task will necessitate a penetrating look at how the defense budgets of today are being assembled and how they can be improved. DOD budget strategy will need to include a combination of savings in some areas, increased investments in others, and smart spending in still others. To forge this strategy, tough decisions will be required on exactly how many funds to commit to each important program and activity. As a consequence, DOD will need to appraise the defense budget in comprehensive terms. An intent focus on the next few years is needed because expeditionary warfare preparedness measures will take shape then. But the long-term procurement effort must also be considered because it will begin to accelerate over the next few years, and decisions made at this time will have an important bearing on how the procurement bow wave is managed throughout the coming 10-15 years. As DOD adopts this integrated approach to the future, it will need to focus on the connections among military strategy, forces, programs, and budgets— a focus that is easily lost at the juncture when strategic planning gives way to handling the myriad details of annual programs and budgets.

Reorganizing the Defense Budget

Recently senior DOD officials improved the PPBES (planning, programming, budgeting, and execution system) by creating more time for in-depth analysis. Joint military processes for reviewing requirements and priorities for capability improvements also have been strengthened. Even so, a major drawback is that the defense budget remains arrayed in categories that inhibit efforts to analyze the relationship between resource inputs and strategic outputs. This problem could be lessened by organizing the program budget into new categories that are aligned with modern-era missions, not those of the Cold War. Figure 1 is an illustrative new categorization scheme of 11 programs that focus on how forces and activities perform key missions. The first three programs focus on conventional combat forces and their missions: joint expeditionary forces, major theater war forces, and special operations forces. These three categories blend active forces and reserve forces together, rather than the current approach of treating them separately. Program 4 combines airlift and sealift forces along with overseas prepositioning. An important innovation is Program 5, which addresses overseas forces and activities. Program 6 postulates that strategic nuclear forces and missile defenses should be treated as a single entity for budgetary purposes. Programs 7-11 array various types of support activities while treating medical programs as a separate entity.[10]

Figure 1. Toward a New Program Budget

Program 1: Joint Expeditionary Forces
Program 2: Major Theater War Forces
Program 3: Special Operations Forces
Program 4: Mobility Forces
Program 5: Forward Presence and International Activities
Program 6: Strategic Nuclear Forces and Missile Defense
Program 7: C4ISR Assets and Activities
Program 8: Research and Development
Program 9: Medical Programs
Program 10: Central Supply, Maintenance, and Installations
Program 11: Personnel, Training, and Development

Parallel steps could be taken to rearrange how the line-item budget is arrayed. Figure 2 is one such example of a new scheme. It combines pay for military personnel and civilian personnel into a single category. It replaces the O&M budget with a new "Operations Budget" that no longer contains civilian pay and is divided into two categories: active force operations and other operations. It divides the procurement budget into two categories: major weapon systems and secondary items. It divides the RDT&E budget into two categories: initial R&D and later RDT&E. The overall effect is to better illuminate how the defense budget is spent and how its various categories perform functions and produce outputs.

---

[10] For more detail, see Stuart Johnson, "A New PPB Process to Advance Transformation," *Defense Horizons* 32 (Washington D.C., Center for Technology and National Security Studies of National Defense University, September, 2003).

Figure 2. Toward a New Line-Item Budget

Military and Civilian Personnel
      Military Pay
      Civilian Pay
Operations Budget
      Active Force Operations
      Other Operations
Procurement
      Major Weapon Systems
      Secondary Items
RDT&E
      Initial R&D
      Later RDT&E
Construction and Housing
      Construction
      Housing
Other

Importance of Analyzing Tradeoffs

DOD will need to engage in the difficult task of assessing cross-program tradeoffs to forge an effective and efficient defense budget strategy. The practice of allocating funds on a business-as-usual basis will not work in the years ahead. When tradeoffs make sense, they should be pursued even if they are unsettling. The idea of using tradeoffs that generate savings to create an annual $15-20 billion funding wedge for expeditionary warfare and related measures sounds daunting, but it would necessitate shifting only 5 percent of today's budget, a manageable task. Likewise the idea of fitting a multi-weapon modernization effort into a procurement budget that may be 10-15 percent short of perfection also sounds daunting. But it also is a manageable task if plans are forged soon, rather than delayed until a massive procurement effort has been launched that must later be ratcheted and reconfigured in disruptive ways. If constraints on DOD procurement plans must be imposed, they are best decided in advance, rather than addressed later in ways that may produce costly cancellations and pare-backs that result in wasting of critical funds or unbalanced modernization programs.

Because future funds may be tight, affordability as well as performance will need to be governing criteria for all programs; critical decisions will be both strategic and economic in character. The task of shaping new allocation strategies will require detailed appraisals using cost and performance data beyond those available from published budget documents. DOD should continue its ongoing efforts to develop new, better performance measures that relate budget inputs to military outputs. It will need to judge all programs and activities not only on the basis of whether they attain their goals, but also on whether they take too many funds away from other, higher-priority endeavors. Because budget savings are needed to pursue expeditionary warfare and long-term transformation, they seemingly are best found in support programs as well as in the O&M budget and some aspects of other budget categories. DOD needs to develop a strategic theory for O&M

spending; it can no longer afford to know the least about its biggest expenditure. Any quest for savings in O&M or elsewhere should be guided by realization that the goal is to transfer funds to higher-leverage enterprises. Such transfers should be guided by the concept that the marginal returns must always match or exceed the opportunity cost.

DOD cannot aspire to a pristine budget in which all funds are so perfectly allocated that any further tradeoffs would result in more losses than gains. But it can aspire to budgets that spend funds as wisely as humanly possible. Creating such budgets will require systematic analysis, including study of preparedness goals, tradeoffs, and risks. Some critics say that serious analysis is not needed when defense budgets are soaring upward and no tough choices must be made. But serious analysis is needed when budgets flatten, requirements grow, and tough choices beckon. Such a time is arriving.

A Comprehensive National Security Budget

A case can be made that the time has arrived to create an overall national security budget that combines the budgets of all departments and agencies in the national security arena. National security is no longer the sole province of defense preparedness. Homeland security, parts of the energy budget, and foreign policy instruments that include diplomatic activities and economic assistance play important roles, too. So does the intelligence community, whose expenses are distributed among multiple agencies. The amount of national security funds spent each year by the Departments of State, Homeland Security, Energy, and the CIA and other agencies is large.

The budgets of these multiple agencies are listed in OMB documents that allow total expenditures to be determined. Some observers argue that budgets from these agencies need to be brought together to form an integrated whole, to be internally coordinated, and to be blended with that of DOD to create a common strategic approach to national security policy and strategy. Those who argue against this step assert that it will not improve management within each agency, and that it could result in unwise spending reductions, especially in the cases of the State Department or DOD. These tradeoffs will need to be addressed if the idea of creating a national security budget gains momentum.

What steps can be taken to begin creating a national security budget? The idea of creating a fully integrated, multi-departmental budget anytime soon may be too ambitious. The attempt would trigger a time-consuming upheaval by requiring many departments to alter their budgetary accounting systems, and by requiring Congress to alter its committee structures and processes for budgetary review. But the simple act of displaying the various departmental budgets side-by-side might provide a better sense of the strategic whole. When the White House issues its national security strategy, it could include budgetary materials from DOD and other agencies that, taken together, form a composite picture. Likewise, each February the President could send a composite national security budget to Congress that includes not only the DOD budget request, but also relevant budgetary programs from other agencies. Eventually, these displays could be improved by providing integrated approaches with common goals and commensurate performance metrics. Creating a national security budget of this sort will not be free of controversy. But in today's world, it may be a worthy idea if its problems can be overcome.

Conclusion

A long-term view of future defense spending is needed. This is the case not only because defense budget growth may level off in the coming years, but also because defense requirements are growing due to the interaction of expeditionary operations in the GWOT and the acceleration of long-term transformation. The United States will need to spend enough on defense to meet future requirements for military preparedness. It also will need to spend its scarce defense dollars as wisely as possible. Even as its carries out demanding operations abroad, it will need to increase its investment spending on procurement so that transformation succeeds. To do so, DOD may need to tighten its belt elsewhere; O&M spending is one example, and there may be others. The future demands not only strategic vision, but also careful analysis.